This book belongs to

_____

This book is dedicated to my children - Mikey, Kobe, and Jojo.

Copyright © Grow Grit Press LLC. All rights reserved. No part of this book may be reproduced in any form without permission in writing from the publisher. Please send bulk order requests to info@ninjalifehacks.tv 978-1-63731-197-4 Printed and bound in the USA. NinjaLifeHacks.tv

Ninja Life Hacks®
by Mary Nhin

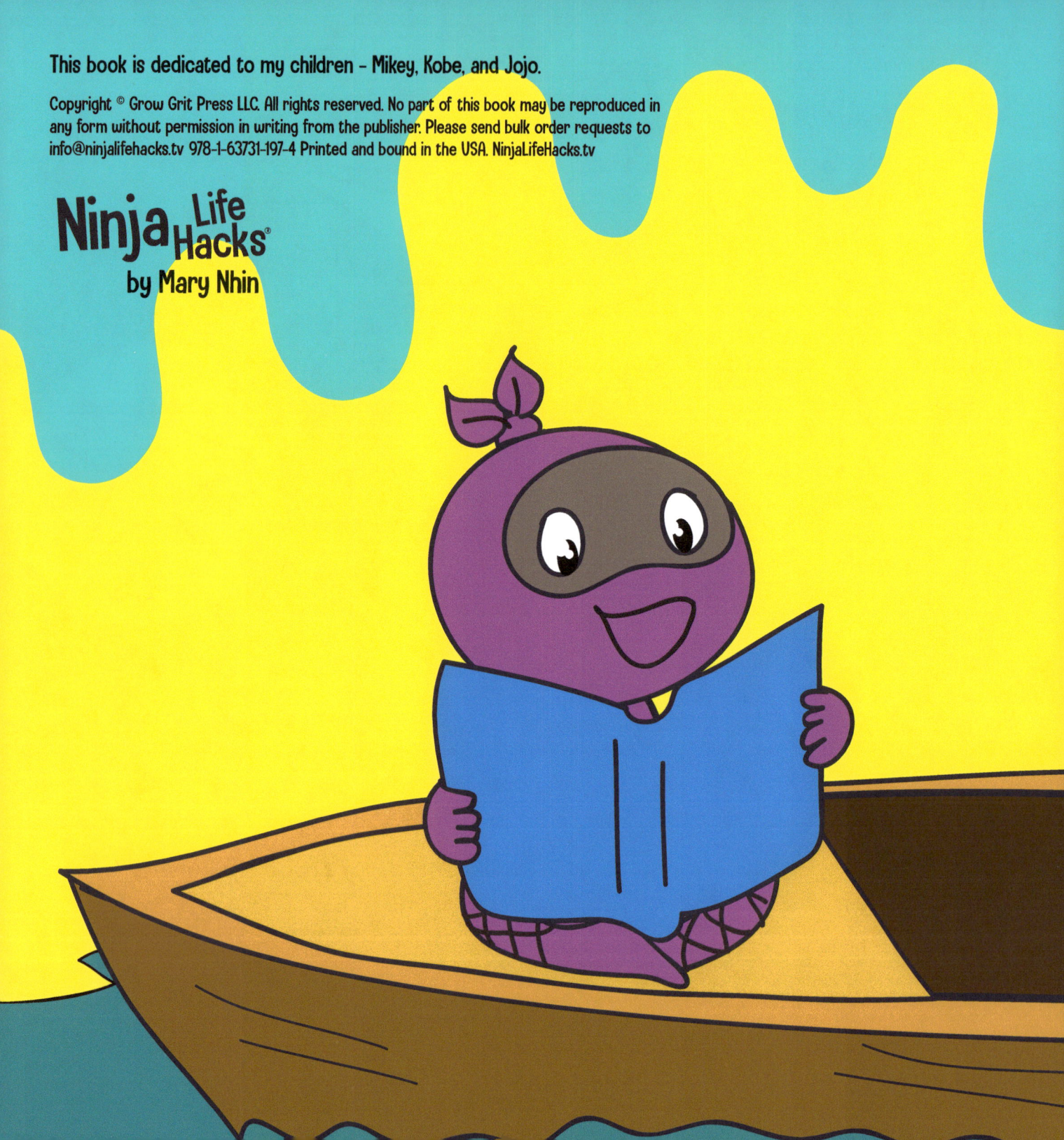

Adaptable Ninja

A Children's Book About Cognitive Flexibility and Set Shifting Skills

Ninja Life Hacks
by Mary Nhin

Hi! I'm Adaptable Ninja.

I use my adaptability skills to accept a change in events or schedule. When we can let go of the old way of doing something in order to use a new way, this is called set shifting.

I haven't always been this adaptable.

I used to be a rigid thinker. When something changed in my normal routine or I had to switch tasks, I felt like the room had turned upside down.

Like yesterday, I was getting ready for my basketball game. Then, my mom told me it was canceled because of the rain. I got so upset!

It wasn't until my friend, Flexible Thinking Ninja, showed me how to be more like water that I became more adaptable in my thinking.

What does being adaptable mean?

Adaptability is a skill that means we can handle change well. We can understand this skill when we compare water to ice.

Ice is hard and inflexible.

Water is flexible and is able to change its shape.

Being like water means we go with the flow even when our expectations change. This skill helps us tolerate changes that may occur. It allows us to accept and create alternative solutions.

Think about the way water moves. When water travels, it can find many different paths. Water is adaptable and will flow in several directions. It will find endless ways to overcome obstacles.

Ice is rigid. If it meets an obstacle, it cannot move past it. Ice is like being unwilling to change. Eventually, the ice will melt, but it will take some time.

When we're adaptable, we have the ability to find more paths to a solution. We can see from multiple perspectives.

But even if we struggle with adaptability, we can work to improve this skill. Just like ice, we can melt into water.

Take what happened to me yesterday as an example.

I had a basketball game. I was so excited about going and playing with my teammates. Then, it started raining and I got upset when my mom told me it was canceled. She suggested we do something else.

Remembering to be more like water could help you become more adaptable!

Check out the Adaptable Ninja lesson plans that contain fun activities to support the social, emotional lesson in this story at ninjalifehacks.tv!

I love to hear from my readers.
Write to me at info@ninjalifehacks.tv or send me mail at:

Mary Nhin
6608 N Western Avenue #1166
Oklahoma City, OK 73116

 @officialninjalifehacks

 Mary Nhin   Ninja Life Hacks

 @marynhin @officialninjalifehacks
#NinjaLifeHacks

 Ninja Life Hacks

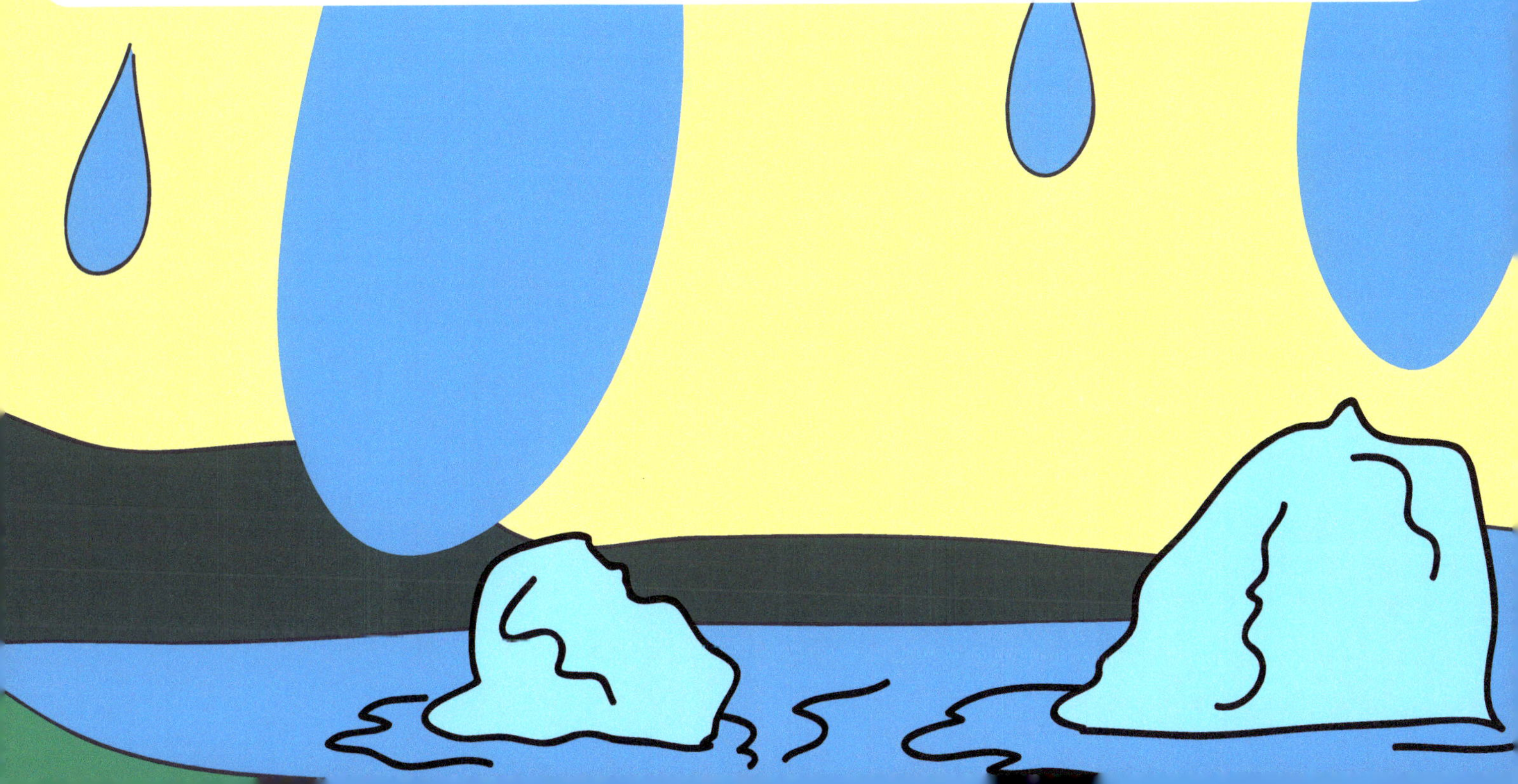

www.ingramcontent.com/pod-product-compliance
Lightning Source LLC
Chambersburg PA
CBHW041524070526
44585CB00002B/67